Mastering Canva

A Comprehensive Guide for Social Media Content Creation

Emily James

able of Conτents

Introduction

Hey there! Welcome to "Mastering Canva: A Comprehensive Guide for Social Media Content Creation". If you've ever found yourself scrolling through Instagram or Facebook and wondering how those stunning visuals come together, you're in the right place. This book is your ticket to mastering Canva, a powerful yet super user-friendly design tool that will transform the way you create content.

Why This Book?

In a world where attention spans are short and the competition for eyeballs is fierce, having eye-catching visuals is no longer a luxury – it's a necessity. Whether you're a small business owner trying to stand out, a freelancer looking to wow your clients, or someone who's just passionate about creating beautiful content, Canva is the perfect tool to help you shine.

But why Canva, you ask? Because it's designed for everyone. You don't need a degree in graphic design to make magic happen with Canva. With its drag-and-drop simplicity and a treasure trove of templates, fonts, and images, Canva makes it possible for anyone to create professional-quality designs.

What's Inside?

This book is packed with everything you need to know about Canva and how to use it to create amazing social media content. Here's a sneak peek at what you'll discover in each chapter:

Chapter 1: Introduction to Canva for Social Media Content Creation

- *What is Canva?*
- *Why use Canva for Social Media Content Creation*
- *Target Audience for this book*

Chapter 2: Getting Started with Canva

- *Creating a Canva account*
- *Navigating the Canva interface*
- *Understanding Canva tools and features*

Chapter 3: Basic Design Principles for Social Media Content

- *Color theory and palettes*
- *Typography tips*
- *Image selection and editing*

Chapter 4: Creating Engaging Social Media Graphics

- *Designing quote graphics*
- *Tips for creating infographics*
- *Crafting eye-catching social media posts*

Chapter 5: Advanced Design Techniques in Canva

- *Using Canva templates effectively*
- *Incorporating animation and video into your designs*
- *Collaborating with team members on Canva*

Chapter 6: Social Media Branding with Canva

- *Establishing a consistent brand identity*
- *Creating branded templates for social media*
- *Designing branded marketing materials*

Chapter 7: Optimizing Social Media Content for Different Platforms

- *Understanding platform-specific design requirements*
- *Tailoring content for Facebook, Instagram, Twitter, LinkedIn, and Pinterest*
- *Scheduling and publishing content from Canva*

Chapter 8: Measuring Success and Iterating on Designs

- *Analyzing social media analytics*
- *A/B testing designs for engagement*
- *Revising and improving social media content*

Chapter 9: Canva for Teams and Collaborative Projects

- *Setting up teams in Canva*
- *Managing permissions and roles*
- *Streamlining communication and feedback processes*

Chapter 10: Conclusion and Next Steps

- *Recap of key concepts*
- *Resources for further learning*
- *Taking your Canva skills to the next level*
- *Appendix: Canva keyboard shortcuts and tips for efficiency*

Who is This Book For?

This book is for everyone – really. Whether you're a beginner just dipping your toes into the design waters or a seasoned pro looking to sharpen your skills, you'll find valuable insights here. Our audience includes:

- *Small Business Owners: Create stunning visuals that help your business stand out.*
- *Freelancers: Impress your clients with professional-quality designs.*
- *Marketing Professionals: Enhance your campaigns with engaging graphics.*
- *Content Creators: Increase your audience engagement with visually appealing content.*
- *Students: Improve your design skills and build an impressive portfolio.*
- *Nonprofit Organizations: Communicate your message effectively with compelling visuals.*
- *Corporate Employees: Boost your company's brand with consistent, high-quality content.*
- *Job Seekers: Add a valuable skill to your resume to stand out to potential employers.*

Let's Get Started!

I'm thrilled to have you on this journey. Canva has revolutionized the way we create and share visual content, and I can't wait to see how it will transform your work. Whether you're here to boost your business, advance your career, or simply have fun with design, this book is your guide to mastering

Canva and making your social media content truly shine.

So, grab your laptop, a cup of coffee, and let's dive into the world of Canva. Together, we'll turn your creative ideas into reality and make your social media presence more vibrant and impactful than ever before.

Happy designing!

Emily James

Chapter 1: Introduction to Canva for Social Media Content Creation

What is Canva?

Canva is a versatile graphic design platform that empowers users to create stunning visual content for various purposes, including social media, marketing materials, presentations, and more. It offers a wide range of tools, templates, and design elements that make it easy for anyone to create professional-looking designs without the need for advanced design skills. From beginner to advanced users, Canva provides a user-friendly interface that allows for easy customization and creativity.

For small business owners, freelancers, marketing professionals, content creators, students, nonprofit organizations, corporate employees, brand managers, creative professionals, and job seekers, Canva is a valuable tool for creating visually appealing and engaging content. Whether you need to design social media posts, business cards, flyers, or presentations, Canva has you covered with its extensive library of templates and design elements. With Canva, you can easily customize your designs to reflect your brand identity and communicate your message effectively.

In the realm of social media content creation in Canva, users can take their designs to the next level by exploring advanced features such as animation, video editing, and collaboration tools. With Canva's intuitive drag-and-drop interface, users can easily create eye-catching social media graphics that stand out in a crowded digital landscape. Whether you're looking to promote your products or services, engage with your audience, or drive traffic to your website, Canva provides the tools you need to succeed in the world of social media marketing.

Social media branding in Canva allows users to develop a cohesive and professional brand identity across all their social media platforms. By utilizing Canva's branding tools, users can create consistent visuals that help reinforce their brand message and values. From customizing color palettes and fonts to creating branded templates and graphics, Canva makes it easy for users to maintain a strong and recognizable brand presence online. With Canva, users can elevate their social media branding efforts and create a memorable and impactful brand image that resonates with their target audience.

Whether you're a beginner looking to dip your toes into the world of graphic design or an advanced user seeking to take your designs to the next level, Canva offers a range of features and tools to suit your needs.

With its user-friendly interface, extensive library of templates and design elements, and advanced customization options, Canva is a powerful tool for creating visually stunning and engaging content. From social media content creation to branding, Canva is a valuable resource for individuals and businesses looking to make a lasting impression online.

Why use Canva for Social Media Content Creation?

In today's digital age, social media has become an essential tool for businesses and individuals to connect with their audience, promote their brand, and drive engagement. With the rise of visual content as an effective marketing strategy, creating eye-catching and professional-looking graphics has never been more important. This is where Canva comes in. Canva is a versatile and user-friendly graphic design platform that allows users to easily create stunning visuals for social media, marketing materials, presentations, and more.

One of the main reasons why Canva is the go-to tool for social media content creation is its ease of use. Whether you are a small business owner, freelance designer, marketing professional, content creator, student, nonprofit organization, corporate employee, brand manager, creative professional, or job seeker, Canva offers a wide range of templates, design elements, and customization options that make it easy to create professional-looking graphics in minutes. With Canva, you don't need to be a graphic design expert to create visually appealing content for your social media channels.

Another key advantage of using Canva for social media content creation is its affordability. Canva offers a free version with basic design tools and templates, as well as a paid version with additional features and access to a larger library of design elements. This makes Canva a cost-effective option for individuals and businesses looking to create high-quality graphics without breaking the bank. With Canva, you can save time and money while still producing visually stunning content for your social media channels.

Furthermore, Canva offers a wide range of design tools and features that make it easy to customize your graphics to fit your brand identity. From choosing the right colors and fonts to adding your logo and brand elements, Canva allows you to create cohesive and on-brand visuals for your social media channels. Whether you are creating posts for Instagram, Facebook, Twitter, LinkedIn, or any other social platform, Canva has the tools you need to create engaging and professional-looking content that resonates with your audience.

In conclusion, Canva is a powerful tool for social media content creation that offers a user-friendly interface, affordability, and a wide range of design tools and features. Whether you are a beginner looking to enhance your social media presence or an advanced user looking to take your branding to the next level, Canva has everything you need to create stunning visuals for your social media channels. By mastering Canva, you can elevate your social media content and stand out in a crowded digital landscape.

Target Audience for this Book

The target audience for this book, "Mastering Canva: A Comprehensive Guide for Social Media Content Creation," is diverse and includes small business owners, freelancers, marketing professionals, content creators, students, nonprofit organizations, corporate employees, brand managers, creative professionals, and job seekers. This book is specifically tailored to those who are looking to enhance their skills in social media content creation using Canva, from beginner to advanced levels.

Small business owners will benefit from this book as they can learn how to create visually appealing social media content that will help them stand out in a crowded marketplace. Freelancers and marketing professionals can sharpen their design skills and create engaging visuals for their clients. Content creators will find valuable tips and techniques to elevate their content and increase engagement with their audience.

Students who are studying design, marketing, or communications can use this book as a resource to improve their skills and create impressive portfolios. Nonprofit organizations can learn how to effectively communicate their message through compelling visuals. Corporate employees and brand managers can enhance their brand identity and create consistent branding across all social media platforms.

Creative professionals will find inspiration and new ideas for their projects, while job seekers can add Canva skills to their resume, making them more attractive to potential employers. Whether you are interested in social media content creation in Canva or social media branding in Canva, this book covers a wide range of topics from beginner to advanced levels, providing valuable insights and practical tips to help you master the art of Canva design.

Chapter 2: Getting Started with Canva

Creating a Canva Account

Creating a Canva account is the first step towards mastering the art of social media content creation. Whether you are a small business owner, freelancer, marketing professional, content creator, student, nonprofit organization, corporate employee, brand manager, creative professional, or job seeker, having a Canva account is essential for creating stunning visuals for your social media platforms. In this subchapter, we will guide you through the process of creating a Canva account and getting started on your journey towards becoming a Canva expert.

To create a Canva account, simply visit the Canva website and click on the "Sign up" button. You will be prompted to enter your email address, create a password, and choose a username. Once you have filled in the required information, click on the "Sign up" button to create your account. You may also choose to sign up using your Google or Facebook account for added convenience.

After successfully creating your Canva account, you will be directed to the Canva dashboard where you can start creating your first design. Familiarize yourself with the various features and tools available on Canva, such as templates, elements, text, and images. Take some time to explore the different design options and experiment with creating your own custom designs.

As you begin creating designs on Canva, you will notice how easy and intuitive the platform is to use. Canva offers a wide range of templates for social media content creation, from beginner to advanced levels. Whether you are looking to create a simple Instagram post or a complex infographic, Canva has got you covered. Take advantage of the drag-and-drop interface to customize your designs and make them uniquely yours.

In conclusion, creating a Canva account is the first step towards mastering social media content creation. By following the steps outlined in this subchapter, you will be well on your way to creating visually appealing and engaging content for your social media platforms. Stay tuned for more tips and tricks on how to take your Canva skills to the next level in the following chapters of this comprehensive guide.

Navigating the Canva Interface

Navigating the Canva interface is a crucial skill for anyone looking to create visually stunning and effective social media content. Whether you are a small business owner, freelance designer, marketing professional, content creator, student, nonprofit organization, corporate employee, brand manager, creative professional, or job seeker, mastering the Canva platform can help elevate your brand and message in the digital realm. In this subchapter, we will delve into the key features and functionalities of Canva that will empower you to create engaging and eye-catching designs with ease.

When you first log into Canva, you will be greeted by a user-friendly interface that is designed to streamline the design process. The main dashboard is divided into sections such as templates, designs, images, and more, making it easy to navigate and locate the tools you need. The left-hand panel contains all the design elements you can add to your canvas, from text and shapes to illustrations and icons. The top toolbar provides quick access to essential features like undo/redo, alignment tools, and the ability to upload your images and brand assets.

One of the standout features of Canva is the vast library of templates available for various social media platforms, including Facebook, Instagram, Twitter, LinkedIn, and more. These professionally designed templates serve as a great starting point for your designs and can be customized to suit your brand's aesthetic and messaging. Simply select a template that resonates with your content goals, then drag and drop elements onto the canvas to personalize it with your branding colors, fonts, and imagery.

As you explore the Canva interface, you will discover a plethora of design tools and functionalities that can take your social media content creation to the next level. From advanced text editing options like kerning and line spacing to image editing features like filters and cropping, Canva offers a comprehensive suite of tools to help you bring your creative vision to life. Additionally, the platform's collaboration features allow you to invite team members to work on designs together, making it an ideal tool for collaborative projects and brand consistency.

In conclusion, mastering the Canva interface is essential for anyone looking to create visually appealing and engaging social media content. By familiarizing yourself with the platform's features and functionalities, you can streamline your design process, elevate your brand's visual identity, and stand out in the crowded digital landscape. Whether you are a beginner or advanced user, Canva offers the tools and resources you need to create professional-quality designs that resonate with your target audience. So, dive into the Canva interface and unleash your creativity today!

Understanding Canva Tools and Features

In this subchapter, we will delve into the essential tools and features of Canva that will help you create stunning social media content. Whether you are a small business owner, freelance professional, marketing expert, content creator, student, nonprofit organization, corporate employee, brand manager, creative professional, or job seeker, mastering Canva is essential for your success in the digital age. Understanding the tools and features of Canva will enable you to create visually appealing and engaging content that will resonate with your target audience.

One of the key tools in Canva is the drag-and-drop editor, which allows you to easily create designs by simply dragging and dropping elements onto your canvas. This feature is user-friendly and intuitive, making it easy for beginners to create professional-looking designs without any prior design experience. Additionally, Canva offers a wide range of pre-designed templates that you can customize to suit your brand's style and message. These templates are fully editable, allowing you to change colors, fonts, images, and other elements to create a unique design that reflects your brand identity.

Another important feature of Canva is the library of millions of high-quality images, illustrations, icons, and fonts that you can use in your designs. This extensive library ensures that you have access to a wide range of visual assets to choose from, allowing you to create visually stunning and engaging content. Additionally, Canva offers advanced editing tools such as the ability to crop, resize, rotate, and adjust the transparency of elements in your design. These tools give you greater control over the visual elements in your design, allowing you to create professional-looking content that will stand out on social media platforms.

Furthermore, Canva's collaboration and sharing features make it easy to work with team members, clients, or collaborators on your designs. You can invite others to view or edit your designs in real-time, making it easy to collaborate on projects and receive feedback. Additionally, Canva allows you to publish your designs directly to social media platforms, websites, or print materials, making it easy to share your creations with your audience. These features streamline the design process and make it easy to create and share content that will help you achieve your marketing goals.

In conclusion, understanding the tools and features of Canva is essential for anyone looking to create professional-quality social media content. Whether you are a beginner or an advanced user, mastering Canva will enable you to create visually appealing and engaging designs that will help you stand out in a crowded digital landscape. By leveraging Canva's intuitive drag-and-drop editor, extensive library of visual assets, advanced editing tools, collaboration features, and sharing capabilities, you can create content that will drive engagement, build brand awareness, and achieve your marketing objectives.

Chapter 3: Basic Design Principles for Social Media Content

Color Theory and Palettes

Color theory and palettes play a crucial role in the success of any design project, especially when it comes to creating engaging and visually appealing social media content. Understanding the basics of color theory can help you make informed decisions when selecting colors for your designs in Canva. By mastering the use of color palettes, you can create cohesive and eye-catching visuals that resonate with your target audience.

In the world of social media content creation, color psychology is a powerful tool that can be leveraged to evoke specific emotions and responses from viewers. Different colors have the ability to convey different messages and elicit various reactions, making it essential to choose colors wisely based on the intended message of your content. For example, warm colors like red and orange are often associated with excitement and energy, while cool colors like blue and green evoke feelings of calmness and trust.

When it comes to selecting colors for your designs in Canva, it's important to consider the overall aesthetic and branding of your social media presence. Creating a consistent color palette that aligns with your brand identity can help establish brand recognition and strengthen your visual identity across different platforms. By using Canva's color palette generator and color wheel tools, you can easily create harmonious color schemes that reflect your brand's personality and values.

Experimenting with different color combinations and variations can also help you discover unique and eye-catching design possibilities for your social media content. By understanding the principles of color theory and palettes, you can confidently mix and match colors to create visually striking visuals that stand out in crowded social media feeds. Whether you're a small business owner, freelance designer, or marketing professional, mastering the art of color selection in Canva can elevate your content creation skills and set you apart from the competition.

In conclusion, color theory and palettes are essential components of successful social media content creation in Canva. By understanding the psychological impact of colors, creating consistent brand color palettes, and experimenting with different color combinations, you can elevate the visual appeal of your designs and communicate your message effectively to your target audience. Whether you're a beginner or an advanced user of Canva, incorporating color theory principles into your design process can help you create visually stunning and engaging social media content that resonates with your audience and drives results for your brand.

Typography Tips

Typography is a crucial element in creating visually appealing and effective social media content. In this subchapter, we will explore some valuable typography tips that will help you elevate your designs and make them stand out in the crowded digital landscape. Whether you are a small business owner, freelance designer, marketing professional, content creator, student, nonprofit organization, corporate employee, brand manager, creative professional, or job seeker, mastering typography in Canva will be a valuable skill to have in your arsenal.

When selecting fonts for your social media content, it is essential to choose fonts that are easy to read and align with your brand identity. Avoid using too many different fonts in one design, as this can make your content look cluttered and unprofessional. Stick to two or three complementary fonts that create a cohesive and harmonious look. Experiment with different font pairings to find the perfect combination that suits your brand and message.

Typography hierarchy is another important aspect to consider when designing social media content. Use different font sizes, weights, and styles to create a visual hierarchy that guides the viewer's eye through the content. Headlines should be larger and bolder to grab attention, while body text should be smaller and easier to read. Utilize hierarchy to emphasize key messages, important information, and calls to action in your designs.

Consistency is key when it comes to typography in social media content creation. Establish a set of brand guidelines that include specific fonts, sizes, colors, and styles to maintain a cohesive look across all your designs. Consistent typography helps reinforce brand recognition and creates a sense of professionalism and reliability. Make sure to use the same fonts and styles in all your social media posts, ads, and graphics to build a strong and recognizable brand presence.

Lastly, don't be afraid to experiment and have fun with typography in your Canva designs. Play around with different font styles, sizes, colors, and effects to create unique and eye-catching content that engages your audience. Use typography to express your brand's personality, evoke emotions, and convey your message effectively. With practice and creativity, you can master typography in Canva and take your social media content creation to the next level.

Image Selection and Editing

In the world of social media content creation, selecting and editing images is a crucial step in creating visually appealing and engaging posts. In this subchapter, we will explore the process of image selection and editing using Canva, a powerful online design tool that is perfect for small business owners, freelancers, marketing professionals, content creators, students, nonprofit organizations, corporate employees, brand managers, creative professionals, and job seekers.

When it comes to image selection, it is important to choose high-quality images that are relevant to your brand and message. Canva offers a wide range of stock photos, illustrations, icons, and graphics that you can use to enhance your social media posts. Additionally, you can upload your own images or choose from Canva's extensive library of templates to create custom designs that reflect your unique style and branding.

Once you have selected your images, it is time to edit them to make them stand out and grab the attention of your audience. Canva's editing tools allow you to adjust the brightness, contrast, saturation, and other elements of your images to create a more polished and professional look. You can also add filters, text overlays, shapes, and other design elements to make your images more visually appealing.

In addition to basic editing tools, Canva also offers advanced features such as photo retouching, background removal, and image resizing. These tools can help you create stunning visuals that are sure to impress your followers and increase engagement on your social media platforms. By taking the time to carefully select and edit your images, you can create a cohesive and visually appealing brand image that will set you apart from the competition.

In conclusion, mastering the art of image selection and editing in Canva is essential for creating high-quality social media content that resonates with your audience. Whether you are a small business owner, freelance designer, marketing professional, or aspiring content creator, Canva's intuitive interface and powerful editing tools make it easy to create stunning visuals that will help you stand out in a crowded digital landscape. By incorporating these tips and techniques into your social media strategy, you can elevate your brand and connect with your audience in a meaningful and impactful way.

Chapter 4: Creating Engaging Social Media Graphics

Designing Quote Graphics

In the world of social media content creation, designing visually appealing and shareable graphics is essential for engaging with your audience. One powerful tool for creating stunning graphics is Canva. In this subchapter, we will delve into the art of designing quote graphics using Canva, a popular graphic design platform that offers a wide range of tools and templates to help you bring your ideas to life.

When designing quote graphics, it is important to choose a visually appealing font that complements the message of the quote. Canva offers a variety of fonts to choose from, ranging from elegant script fonts to bold sans-serif fonts. Experiment with different font styles and sizes to find the perfect combination that enhances the overall look of your design.

Another key element in designing quote graphics is selecting the right background image or color. Canva provides a vast library of stock photos, illustrations, and background colors to choose from. Consider the mood and tone of the quote when selecting a background image or color to ensure that it complements the message you are trying to convey.

In addition to font selection and background choices, you can further enhance your quote graphics by adding decorative elements such as shapes, icons, and borders. Canva offers a wide range of design elements that you can use to add visual interest and personality to your graphics. Experiment with different combinations of elements to create a unique and eye-catching design.

Once you have finalized your quote graphic design, you can easily share it on social media platforms such as Instagram, Facebook, and Twitter directly from Canva. By mastering the art of designing quote graphics in Canva, you can elevate your social media content and engage with your audience in a meaningful and impactful way.

Tips for Creating Infographics

Creating infographics is an essential skill for anyone involved in social media content creation, branding, or marketing. Infographics are visually appealing and easily shareable, making them a powerful tool for conveying information in a concise and engaging way. In this subchapter, we will discuss some key tips for creating effective infographics using Canva, a popular graphic design tool that is user-friendly and versatile.

First and foremost, it is important to have a clear objective in mind when creating an infographic. What message do you want to convey? Who is your target audience? Answering these questions will help you determine the content and design elements that are most relevant and impactful for your infographic. Keep your message focused and concise, as cluttered or confusing infographics are less likely to be well-received.

When selecting colors and fonts for your infographic, consider your brand identity and the preferences of your target audience. Use colors that complement each other and enhance readability, and choose fonts that are easy to read and align with your brand's aesthetic. Canva offers a wide range of pre-designed templates and color palettes to help you create a cohesive and visually appealing infographic.

Visual elements such as icons, illustrations, and charts can enhance the overall impact of your infographic. Use these elements strategically to break up text, highlight key points, and engage your audience. Canva provides a library of free and premium graphic assets that you can easily incorporate into your design. Experiment with different layouts and arrangements to find the most effective visual hierarchy for your infographic.

Lastly, remember to optimize your infographic for social media sharing. Make sure your design is mobile-friendly and easily downloadable. Include your logo or website URL to drive traffic back to your brand. Consider creating multiple versions of your infographic for different social media platforms, as optimal image sizes and formats may vary. By following these tips and leveraging the features of Canva, you can create professional and engaging infographics that effectively communicate your message and elevate your brand presence online.

Crafting Eye-catching Social Media Posts

Crafting eye-catching social media posts is essential for engaging your audience and driving traffic to your website or business. In this subchapter, we will explore some tips and techniques for creating visually appealing posts that will capture the attention of your followers.

First and foremost, it is important to understand your target audience and tailor your posts to their preferences. Consider what types of content resonate with them, whether it be inspirational quotes, behind-the-scenes glimpses, or product showcases. By understanding your audience, you can create posts that speak directly to their interests and needs.

Next, consider the visual elements of your posts. Use high-quality images, graphics, and videos to grab the attention of your followers. Canva offers a wide range of templates, fonts, and design elements that can help you create professional-looking posts in no time. Experiment with different layouts and color schemes to see what resonates with your audience.

In addition to visuals, don't forget about the importance of compelling copy. Craft catchy headlines and captions that will entice your followers to engage with your posts. Use Canva's text tools to add emphasis and style to your copy, making it stand out from the competition.

Finally, don't be afraid to experiment and try new things. Social media is a constantly evolving landscape, so it's important to stay on top of trends and keep your content fresh and engaging. By experimenting with different types of posts, you can learn what works best for your audience and refine your social media strategy accordingly.

By following these tips and techniques for crafting eye-catching social media posts, you can elevate your online presence and connect with your audience in a meaningful way. Canva provides the tools and resources you need to create stunning visuals that will help you stand out in a crowded digital landscape.

Chapter 5: Advanced Design Techniques in Canva

Using Canva Templates Effectively

In this subchapter, we will explore the various ways in which you can effectively utilize Canva templates to enhance your social media content creation. Canva offers a wide range of professionally designed templates that cater to different industries, styles, and purposes. By leveraging these templates, you can save time and effort in designing high-quality graphics for your social media posts.

First and foremost, it is important to choose a template that aligns with your brand identity and messaging. Whether you are a small business owner, freelance professional, marketer, content creator, student, nonprofit organization, corporate employee, brand manager, creative professional, or job seeker, selecting a template that reflects your brand's colors, fonts, and overall aesthetic will help maintain consistency across your social media channels.

Once you have selected a template, it is essential to customize it to suit your specific needs. Canva allows you to easily edit text, images, colors, and layout to create a unique and eye-catching design. Make sure to replace placeholder text with your own content, upload relevant images, and adjust elements to match your branding guidelines. This personalization will ensure that your social media posts stand out and resonate with your target audience.

Furthermore, don't be afraid to experiment with different templates to find what works best for your social media content. Canva offers a variety of templates for different types of posts, such as quotes, promotions, announcements, and event invitations. By trying out various templates and designs, you can discover what resonates most with your audience and drives engagement on your social media platforms.

In conclusion, mastering the use of Canva templates can significantly enhance your social media content creation efforts. By selecting templates that align with your brand identity, customizing them to suit your specific needs, and experimenting with different designs, you can create visually appealing and engaging graphics for your social media posts. Whether you are a beginner or an advanced user, leveraging Canva templates effectively can help you elevate your social media branding and stand out in the digital landscape.

Incorporating Animation and Video into your Designs

Incorporating animation and video into your designs can significantly enhance the visual appeal and engagement of your social media content. With the rise of video content across various social media platforms, it has become essential for businesses and creators to leverage these tools to stand out in a crowded digital landscape. In this subchapter, we will explore how you can effectively integrate animation and video into your designs using Canva, a user-friendly graphic design platform.

One of the key benefits of incorporating animation and video into your designs is the ability to convey complex messages in a simple and engaging manner. Animated elements can help you break down information into digestible chunks, making it easier for your audience to understand and retain key points. Additionally, videos can help you showcase products or services in a dynamic and interactive way, capturing the attention of your target audience and driving engagement.

When incorporating animation and video into your designs, it is important to maintain a cohesive visual identity across all your content. This includes using consistent colors, fonts, and imagery to ensure that your brand is easily recognizable and memorable to your audience. Canva offers a wide range of customizable templates and design elements that can help you create cohesive and professional-looking animations and videos that align with your brand guidelines.

In addition to enhancing the visual appeal of your content, incorporating animation and video into your designs can also help improve your search engine optimization (SEO) efforts. Video content is highly favored by search engines like Google, making it easier for your content to rank higher in search results. By optimizing your videos with relevant keywords and descriptions, you can increase your visibility and drive more organic traffic to your website or social media profiles.

In conclusion, incorporating animation and video into your designs using Canva can help you create visually appealing and engaging content that resonates with your audience. Whether you are a small business owner, freelancer, marketer, content creator, student, nonprofit organization, corporate employee, brand manager, creative professional, or job seeker, mastering the art of animation and video design can set you apart in the competitive world of social media content creation. Experiment with different animation and video techniques in Canva to discover what works best for your brand and audience, and watch your engagement and visibility soar.

Collaborating with Team Members on Canva

Collaborating with team members on Canva can greatly enhance the efficiency and creativity of your social media content creation process. By working together on the platform, you can easily share ideas, provide feedback, and make real-time edits to designs. This subchapter will guide you through the various features and tools available on Canva for seamless collaboration with your team members.

One of the key features of Canva that facilitates collaboration is the ability to share designs with team members. By simply clicking on the "Share" button, you can invite others to view or edit your design. This feature is particularly useful for small business owners, freelancers, and marketing professionals who need to work together on projects remotely. With Canva, team members can access the same design in real-time and make changes as needed, ensuring that everyone is on the same page.

In addition to sharing designs, Canva also offers a commenting feature that allows team members to provide feedback on specific elements of a design. This feature is invaluable for content creators, students, and nonprofit organizations who rely on constructive criticism to improve their work. By leaving comments directly on the design, team members can communicate their thoughts and suggestions effectively, leading to more polished and professional-looking social media content.

Furthermore, Canva provides a seamless workflow for team collaboration by allowing users to assign roles and permissions to team members. This feature is particularly beneficial for corporate employees, brand managers, and creative professionals who need to maintain control over their designs. By assigning specific roles, such as editor or viewer, you can ensure that team members have the appropriate level of access to the design while protecting sensitive information and maintaining brand consistency.

Overall, collaborating with team members on Canva is a powerful tool for job seekers and individuals looking to enhance their social media content creation skills. By leveraging the platform's sharing, commenting, and role assignment features, you can streamline your workflow, improve communication, and create stunning designs that resonate with your target audience. Whether you are a beginner or an advanced user, Canva offers a user-friendly and intuitive interface that makes collaboration a breeze for all types of users.

Chapter 6: Social Media Branding with Canva

Establishing a Consistent Brand Identity

Establishing a consistent brand identity is crucial for any business looking to make a lasting impression on their target audience. In the world of social media content creation, this becomes even more important as the competition for attention is fierce. As small business owners, freelancers, marketing professionals, content creators, students, nonprofit organizations, corporate employees, brand managers, creative professionals, and job seekers, it is essential to understand the importance of creating a cohesive brand identity across all platforms.

One of the first steps in establishing a consistent brand identity is defining your brand's values, mission, and vision. Understanding what your brand stands for and what sets it apart from competitors will help guide your design choices in Canva. By creating a brand style guide that outlines your brand's color palette, typography, logo usage, and other key elements, you can ensure that all your social media content is cohesive and on-brand.

Consistency is key when it comes to building brand recognition and loyalty. By using Canva's templates and design tools to create branded graphics, posts, and ads, you can maintain a consistent look and feel across all your social media channels. Whether you're creating Instagram posts, Facebook ads, or LinkedIn banners, sticking to your brand's style guide will help reinforce your brand identity and make your content more recognizable to your audience.

Another important aspect of establishing a consistent brand identity is ensuring that your messaging is aligned with your brand values and voice. Whether you're writing captions for your social media posts or creating ad copy for your campaigns, it's essential to maintain a consistent tone that resonates with your target audience. By using Canva's text and editing tools, you can craft compelling, on-brand messaging that reinforces your brand identity and engages your followers.

In conclusion, establishing a consistent brand identity is essential for small business owners, freelancers, marketing professionals, content creators, students, nonprofit organizations, corporate employees, brand managers, creative professionals, and job seekers looking to stand out in the crowded social media landscape. By defining your brand values, creating a brand style guide, maintaining consistency in your design choices, and aligning your messaging with your brand voice, you can create a strong and memorable brand identity that resonates with your audience. Canva's user-friendly design tools make it easy to bring your brand to life across all your social media channels, from beginner to advanced levels.

Creating Branded Templates for Social Media

In today's digital age, creating branded templates for social media is essential for any business or individual looking to establish a strong online presence. By using tools like Canva, you can easily design eye-catching templates that reflect your brand identity and help you stand out in a crowded digital landscape. In this subchapter, we will explore the various ways in which you can create branded templates for social media using Canva, from beginner to advanced techniques.

The first step in creating branded templates for social media is to define your brand identity. This includes your brand colors, fonts, logos, and overall aesthetic. By establishing a cohesive brand identity, you can ensure that your templates are consistent across all platforms and easily recognizable to your audience. Canva offers a wide range of customization options, allowing you to easily incorporate your brand elements into your templates.

Once you have defined your brand identity, you can start creating templates for your social media posts. Canva offers a variety of pre-designed templates for various social media platforms, including Facebook, Instagram, Twitter, and Pinterest. You can customize these templates to fit your brand by changing the colors, fonts, and images to align with your brand identity. Additionally, you can create your own templates from scratch using Canva's intuitive design tools.

When creating branded templates for social media, it's important to keep your audience in mind. Consider the type of content that resonates with your target audience and tailor your templates to appeal to their interests and preferences. By creating templates that are relevant and engaging to your audience, you can increase the likelihood of your content being shared and reaching a wider audience. Canva's design tools make it easy to create visually appealing templates that will capture the attention of your followers.

In conclusion, creating branded templates for social media is a powerful way to establish a strong online presence and build brand recognition. By using Canva's design tools, you can easily create templates that reflect your brand identity and help you stand out in a crowded digital landscape. Whether you are a small business owner, freelance professional, marketing professional, or student, mastering the art of creating branded templates for social media in Canva can take your social media content creation to the next level.

Designing Branded Marketing Materials

In the world of marketing, creating visually appealing and cohesive branded materials is essential for establishing a strong brand identity and attracting the attention of your target audience. Designing branded marketing materials is a crucial step in building brand recognition and credibility. In this subchapter, we will explore the key principles and best practices for designing branded marketing materials using Canva, a versatile and user-friendly design tool.

When designing branded marketing materials, it is important to start by defining your brand's visual identity. This includes your brand colors, fonts, logo, and any other visual elements that are unique to your brand. By consistently using these elements across all your marketing materials, you will create a cohesive and recognizable brand image that will resonate with your audience.

One of the key advantages of using Canva for designing branded marketing materials is its wide range of customizable templates. Canva offers a variety of templates for social media posts, flyers, brochures, business cards, and more, making it easy to create professional-looking materials quickly and efficiently. By customizing these templates with your brand colors, fonts, and imagery, you can ensure that all your marketing materials are consistent with your brand identity.

Another important aspect of designing branded marketing materials is creating visually engaging and high-quality graphics. Canva provides a range of design tools and features that allow you to easily create eye-catching graphics, such as image filters, text effects, and shapes. By incorporating these design elements into your marketing materials, you can enhance the visual appeal of your content and make it more engaging for your audience.

In conclusion, designing branded marketing materials is a critical aspect of building a strong brand identity and attracting the attention of your target audience. By following the key principles and best practices outlined in this subchapter, you can create professional-looking marketing materials that are consistent with your brand identity and effectively communicate your message to your audience. With the help of Canva's versatile design tools and customizable templates, you can easily create visually appealing and engaging branded materials that will help you stand out in a crowded marketplace.

Chapter 7: Optimizing Social Media Content for Different Platforms

Understanding Platform-Specific Design Requirements

Understanding Platform-Specific Design Requirements is crucial when creating social media content in Canva. Each platform has its own unique specifications and guidelines that must be adhered to in order to optimize engagement and reach. Small business owners, freelancers, marketing professionals, content creators, students, nonprofit organizations, corporate employees, brand managers, creative professionals, and job seekers can benefit greatly from understanding these requirements to create impactful and effective designs.

When designing for platforms such as Instagram, Facebook, Twitter, LinkedIn, and Pinterest, it is important to consider the different image sizes, aspect ratios, and file formats that each platform requires. For example, Instagram posts should be square (1080 x 1080 pixels), while Instagram stories should be vertical (1080 x 1920 pixels). By understanding these platform-specific design requirements, users can ensure that their content looks professional and visually appealing on each platform.

In addition to image sizes and aspect ratios, each platform also has its own design elements that should be considered. For example, Instagram is a highly visual platform that thrives on high-quality images and aesthetically pleasing designs. On the other hand, Twitter is more text-based, so users should focus on creating engaging copy and incorporating images or graphics to enhance their tweets. By understanding these platform-specific design requirements, users can tailor their content to best suit the platform and audience they are targeting.

Furthermore, understanding platform-specific design requirements can also help users stay on brand and maintain a cohesive visual identity across all platforms. By using consistent colors, fonts, and design elements, users can create a strong brand presence and increase brand recognition. This is especially important for small business owners, freelancers, and nonprofit organizations who rely on social media to promote their products, services, or causes.

Overall, mastering platform-specific design requirements in Canva is essential for creating successful social media content that resonates with your audience. By understanding image sizes, aspect ratios, design elements, and brand consistency, users can create visually appealing and engaging content that drives traffic, increases engagement, and ultimately helps achieve their goals. Whether you are a beginner or advanced user, taking the time to understand these requirements will greatly benefit your social media content creation efforts.

Tailoring Content for Facebook, Instagram, Twitter, LinkedIn, and Pinterest

In today's digital age, it is essential for businesses and individuals to have a strong presence on social media platforms such as Facebook, Instagram, Twitter, LinkedIn, and Pinterest. However, each platform has its own unique audience and features, so it is important to tailor your content accordingly. In this subchapter, we will discuss how to create engaging and effective content for each of these platforms using Canva.

Facebook is one of the most popular social media platforms, with over 2.8 billion active users. When creating content for Facebook, it is important to keep in mind that visuals are key. Use eye-catching images and videos to grab the attention of your audience. Canva offers a wide range of templates and design tools that can help you create visually appealing content for Facebook posts, ads, and cover photos.

Instagram is a visual platform that is perfect for showcasing products, services, and behind-the-scenes glimpses of your business. When creating content for Instagram, focus on high-quality images and videos that are visually appealing and on-brand. Canva's Instagram templates make it easy to create stunning posts, stories, and IGTV videos that will help you stand out on the platform.

Twitter is a fast-paced platform that is perfect for sharing news, updates, and engaging with your audience in real-time. When creating content for Twitter, keep it short and to the point. Canva's Twitter templates can help you create eye-catching graphics and images that will grab the attention of your followers as they scroll through their feed.

LinkedIn is a professional networking platform that is perfect for showcasing your expertise, connecting with industry professionals, and sharing thought leadership content. When creating content for LinkedIn, focus on creating informative and engaging posts that will resonate with your audience. Canva's LinkedIn templates can help you create professional-looking graphics and presentations that will help you establish your brand as a thought leader in your industry.

Pinterest is a visual search engine that is perfect for driving traffic to your website, blog, or online store. When creating content for Pinterest, focus on creating visually appealing pins that include a clear call-to-action. Canva's Pinterest templates can help you create eye-catching pins that will attract clicks and drive traffic to your website. By tailoring your content for each of these platforms using Canva, you can create engaging and effective social media content that will help you reach your target audience and achieve your business goals.

Scheduling and Publishing Content from Canva

Scheduling and publishing content from Canva is an essential aspect of effective social media management. By utilizing Canva's scheduling and publishing features, small business owners, freelancers, marketing professionals, content creators, students, nonprofit organizations, corporate employees, brand managers, creative professionals, and job seekers can streamline their workflow and ensure consistent and timely delivery of content to their audience.

One of the key benefits of using Canva for scheduling and publishing content is the ability to plan and organize your social media posts in advance. By creating a content calendar within Canva, users can easily map out their content strategy, schedule posts for specific dates and times, and ensure a steady flow of engaging and relevant content for their audience. This feature is particularly useful for busy professionals who may not have the time to manually post content each day.

In addition to scheduling content, Canva also offers a variety of publishing options to help users reach their target audience more effectively. From directly posting to social media platforms such as Facebook, Instagram, Twitter, and LinkedIn to exporting designs for use in email campaigns or on websites, Canva provides a seamless integration with popular digital marketing channels. This allows users to maximize their reach and engagement by tailoring their content for each specific platform.

Furthermore, Canva's scheduling and publishing tools include analytics and reporting features that allow users to track the performance of their content and make data-driven decisions to optimize their social media strategy. By monitoring key metrics such as engagement, reach, and click-through rates, users can identify trends, measure the impact of their content, and make adjustments to improve their overall digital marketing efforts.

Overall, mastering the art of scheduling and publishing content from Canva is essential for anyone looking to elevate their social media presence and effectively engage with their target audience. By leveraging Canva's intuitive tools and features, users can create, schedule, and publish high-quality content that resonates with their followers and drives meaningful results for their business or personal brand.

Chapter 8: Measuring Success and Iterating on Designs

Analyzing Social Media Analytics

In today's digital age, social media analytics play a crucial role in understanding the performance of your content and engagement with your audience. Analyzing social media analytics can provide valuable insights into the effectiveness of your social media marketing efforts. This subchapter will delve into the various metrics and tools available to help you make informed decisions and optimize your social media content strategy.

One of the key metrics to analyze in social media analytics is engagement. Engagement metrics such as likes, comments, shares, and clicks can provide valuable insights into how your audience is interacting with your content. By tracking these metrics, you can identify which types of content resonate most with your audience and tailor your content strategy accordingly.

Another important metric to analyze is reach and impressions. Reach refers to the number of unique users who have seen your content, while impressions refer to the total number of times your content has been viewed. By analyzing reach and impressions, you can gauge the overall visibility of your content and determine the effectiveness of your social media campaigns in reaching your target audience.

Furthermore, analyzing social media analytics can help you track the performance of your social media ads. By examining metrics such as click-through rate, conversion rate, and cost per acquisition, you can assess the effectiveness of your ad campaigns and make data-driven decisions to optimize your ad performance and drive better results.

In conclusion, analyzing social media analytics is essential for small business owners, freelancers, marketing professionals, content creators, students, nonprofit organizations, corporate employees, brand managers, creative professionals, and job seekers. By understanding and interpreting the various metrics available, you can gain valuable insights into the performance of your social media content and campaigns, and make informed decisions to improve your social media strategy and achieve your marketing goals.

A/B Testing Designs for Engagement

In the world of social media content creation, engagement is key. Whether you are a small business owner, freelance designer, marketing professional, content creator, student, nonprofit organization, corporate employee, brand manager, creative professional, or job seeker, understanding how to design content that resonates with your audience is essential. A/B testing designs for engagement is a powerful strategy that can help you optimize your social media content and drive better results.

A/B testing involves creating two different versions of a design and testing them to see which one performs better in terms of engagement metrics such as likes, shares, comments, and click-through rates. By comparing the performance of the two designs, you can identify which elements are most effective in capturing your audience's attention and driving them to take action. This data-driven approach allows you to make informed decisions about your design choices and continuously improve the effectiveness of your social media content.

When conducting A/B testing for engagement, it is important to focus on specific design elements that can impact user behavior. These elements may include color schemes, fonts, imagery, layout, call-to-action buttons, and overall messaging. By testing variations of these elements, you can gain valuable insights into what resonates with your audience and drives them to engage with your content. This iterative process of testing and refining your designs can lead to significant improvements in your social media engagement rates over time.

In order to conduct A/B testing for engagement effectively, it is important to establish clear goals and metrics for success. Determine what specific engagement metrics you want to improve, such as increasing likes by 10%, doubling the number of shares, or tripling click-through rates. By setting measurable goals, you can track the impact of your A/B tests and make data-driven decisions about which design elements are most effective in driving engagement with your audience.

In conclusion, A/B testing designs for engagement is a valuable strategy for optimizing your social media content and driving better results. By testing variations of your designs and analyzing the performance data, you can identify what resonates with your audience and make informed decisions about your design choices. Whether you are a beginner or advanced user of Canva, incorporating A/B testing into your design process can help you create more engaging and effective social media content that drives results for your business or organization.

Revising and Improving Social Media Content

In the world of social media, creating engaging and visually appealing content is crucial for capturing the attention of your audience. However, simply creating content is not enough. It is important to continuously revise and improve your social media content to ensure that it remains relevant and effective. In this subchapter, we will discuss some tips and strategies for revising and improving your social media content using Canva.

One of the first steps in revising and improving your social media content is to analyze the performance of your existing content. Take a look at which posts have generated the most engagement and which ones have fallen flat. By understanding what is resonating with your audience, you can tailor your future content to better meet their needs and preferences.

Another key aspect of revising and improving social media content is to ensure that it is visually appealing. Use Canva's design tools to create eye-catching graphics, infographics, and videos that will grab the attention of your audience. Experiment with different colors, fonts, and layouts to find what works best for your brand.

It is also important to keep your content fresh and up-to-date. Regularly update your social media profiles with new content and information to keep your audience engaged. Consider creating a content calendar to plan out your posts in advance and ensure that you are consistently posting high-quality content.

Lastly, don't be afraid to experiment and try new things with your social media content. Use Canva's templates and design tools to create unique and innovative content that will set your brand apart from the competition. By continuously revising and improving your social media content, you can ensure that your brand stays relevant and continues to grow in the ever-changing digital landscape.

Chapter 9: Canva for Teams and Collaborative Projects

Setting Up Teams in Canva

In the world of social media content creation, collaboration is key to success. Canva, a powerful design tool, offers the ability to set up teams to work together seamlessly on projects. In this subchapter, we will discuss the benefits of setting up teams in Canva and provide step-by-step instructions on how to do so effectively.

Setting up teams in Canva allows small business owners, freelancers, marketing professionals, content creators, students, nonprofit organizations, corporate employees, brand managers, creative professionals, and job seekers to work together in a centralized platform. This streamlines the design process, enhances communication, and ensures consistency in branding and messaging across all social media channels.

To get started, simply log in to your Canva account and navigate to the "Teams" tab. From there, you can create a new team by entering a team name and inviting members via email. You can also assign roles to team members, such as "Admin" or "Member," to control access to projects and assets within the team.

Once your team is set up, you can easily collaborate on designs by sharing templates, images, and other assets with team members. This allows for real-time feedback and edits, ensuring that everyone is on the same page and working towards a cohesive final product. Additionally, you can create folders to organize projects and assets within the team, making it easy to find and access files when needed.

Overall, setting up teams in Canva is a game-changer for social media content creation. It allows for seamless collaboration, improved communication, and enhanced efficiency in the design process. Whether you are a beginner or an advanced user of Canva, utilizing teams can take your social media branding to the next level. So, gather your team and start creating stunning designs that will elevate your online presence and engage your audience like never before.

Managing Permissions and Roles

In the world of social media content creation, managing permissions and roles is crucial for ensuring smooth collaboration and organization within a team or organization. In this subchapter, we will delve into the important aspects of permissions and roles in Canva, a powerful design tool that can help streamline your social media content creation process.

Permissions in Canva refer to the level of access and control that users have over a specific design or project. As a small business owner, freelance professional, or marketing professional, it is essential to assign the appropriate permissions to team members based on their role and responsibilities. This ensures that sensitive information and brand assets are protected while allowing team members to collaborate effectively.

Roles, on the other hand, define the specific responsibilities and tasks that each team member is assigned within Canva. Whether you are a content creator, student, nonprofit organization, corporate employee, brand manager, creative professional, or job seeker, understanding your role within a project is essential for ensuring that tasks are completed efficiently and effectively. Canva offers a range of roles such as Owner, Admin, and Member, each with specific permissions and capabilities.

By effectively managing permissions and roles in Canva, you can streamline your social media content creation process and improve collaboration within your team. As a small business owner or freelance professional, this can help you ensure that your brand assets are protected and that your content is created in a timely manner. For marketing professionals, content creators, students, nonprofit organizations, corporate employees, brand managers, creative professionals, and job seekers, understanding how to manage permissions and roles in Canva can enhance your workflow and productivity.

In conclusion, mastering the art of managing permissions and roles in Canva is essential for anyone involved in social media content creation. By assigning the appropriate permissions and roles to team members, you can ensure that projects are completed efficiently, brand assets are protected, and collaboration is streamlined. Whether you are a small business owner, freelance professional, marketing professional, content creator, student, nonprofit organization, corporate employee, brand manager, creative professional, or job seeker, understanding how to manage permissions and roles in Canva is a valuable skill that can benefit your social media content creation efforts.

Streamlining Communication and Feedback Processes

In today's fast-paced digital world, effective communication and feedback processes are essential for success in social media content creation. Streamlining these processes can help small business owners, freelancers, marketing professionals, content creators, students, nonprofit organizations, corporate employees, brand managers, creative professionals, and job seekers achieve their goals more efficiently. By mastering the art of communication and feedback in Canva, you can create high-quality content that resonates with your audience and drives results.

One key aspect of streamlining communication and feedback processes is establishing clear channels for collaboration. Whether you are working with a team or creating content solo, having a designated platform for sharing ideas, providing feedback, and making revisions is crucial. Canva's collaboration features, such as commenting and sharing links, make it easy to communicate with others and keep track of changes in real-time. By utilizing these tools effectively, you can ensure that everyone is on the same page and working towards a common goal.

Another important factor in streamlining communication and feedback processes is setting clear expectations and guidelines. Establishing a communication plan that outlines roles, responsibilities, deadlines, and feedback protocols can help minimize confusion and ensure that everyone is working towards a common vision. By creating a structured framework for communication, you can streamline the feedback process and avoid misunderstandings that can lead to delays or errors in your content creation.

In addition to clear communication and feedback processes, it is also essential to prioritize active listening and constructive feedback. Encouraging open dialogue and welcoming diverse perspectives can lead to more innovative ideas and better outcomes. By actively listening to feedback from others and incorporating their suggestions into your work, you can improve the quality of your content and enhance your overall creative process.

In conclusion, streamlining communication and feedback processes is essential for success in social media content creation. By establishing clear channels for collaboration, setting expectations and guidelines, and prioritizing active listening and constructive feedback, you can create high-quality content that engages your audience and drives results. Mastering these skills in Canva will not only improve your content creation process but also help you stand out in a competitive digital landscape.

Chapter 10: Conclusion and Next Steps

Recap of Key Concepts

In this subchapter, we will recap some of the key concepts covered in the book "Mastering Canva: A Comprehensive Guide for Social Media Content Creation." Whether you are a small business owner, freelance professional, marketing expert, content creator, student, nonprofit organization, corporate employee, brand manager, creative professional, or job seeker, understanding these key concepts will help you excel in creating stunning social media content using Canva.

First and foremost, it is important to understand the basics of Canva and how to navigate the platform efficiently. Familiarize yourself with the various tools and features available, such as templates, images, text options, and design elements. By mastering the basics, you can streamline your workflow and create polished content in a fraction of the time.

Next, let's delve into the importance of branding in social media content creation. Establishing a strong and consistent brand identity is essential for building brand recognition and trust among your target audience. Use Canva to customize your designs with your brand colors, fonts, logos, and imagery to create a cohesive and professional look across all your social media platforms.

Additionally, mastering the art of visual storytelling is crucial for engaging your audience and conveying your message effectively. Use Canva's design tools to create visually appealing graphics, infographics, and videos that tell a compelling story and resonate with your audience. Incorporate storytelling techniques such as using captivating visuals, compelling headlines, and concise messaging to grab your audience's attention and keep them engaged.

Furthermore, understanding the principles of effective design and layout can make a significant difference in the impact of your social media content. Learn about design elements such as balance, contrast, hierarchy, alignment, and whitespace to create visually appealing and easy-to-read designs. Experiment with different layouts, fonts, colors, and imagery to find the perfect combination that best conveys your message and captures your audience's attention.

Lastly, don't forget the importance of staying updated on the latest trends and best practices in social media content creation. Follow industry experts, attend workshops and webinars, and continuously refine your skills to stay ahead of the curve. By implementing these key concepts and strategies in your social media content creation using Canva, you can elevate your brand, engage your audience, and achieve your marketing goals effectively.

Resources for Further Learning

For those looking to expand their knowledge and skills in social media content creation using Canva, there are a plethora of resources available to help you on your journey. Whether you are a small business owner, freelance professional, marketing expert, content creator, student, nonprofit organization, corporate employee, brand manager, creative professional, or job seeker, these resources are tailored to meet your specific needs and goals in mastering Canva.

One of the first resources you may want to explore is online courses dedicated to Canva and social media content creation. Platforms like Udemy, Skillshare, and Coursera offer a variety of courses ranging from beginner to advanced levels. These courses cover topics such as graphic design principles, branding strategies, social media marketing, and more. By enrolling in these courses, you can gain a deeper understanding of how to leverage Canva for your social media branding efforts.

Another valuable resource for further learning is Canva's own online tutorials and resources. The Canva Design School provides a wealth of information on how to use the platform effectively, including tips and tricks for creating stunning social media graphics. Additionally, Canva's blog and social media channels regularly feature tutorials, case studies, and design inspiration to help you stay up-to-date on the latest trends in social media content creation.

Books and e-books are also great resources for those looking to enhance their skills in Canva and social media branding. There are numerous titles available that cover topics such as visual storytelling, content marketing, branding, and design principles. Some recommended books include "Canva for Work: Quick Start Guide" by George B. Thomas and "The Content Code: Six Essential Strategies to Ignite Your Content, Your Marketing, and Your Business" by Mark W. Schaefer.

Lastly, networking with other professionals in the industry can be a valuable resource for further learning. Joining online communities, attending workshops and conferences, and participating in webinars can help you connect with like-minded individuals and gain insights from experts in the field. By immersing yourself in a community of fellow Canva users and social media content creators, you can expand your knowledge, skills, and opportunities for growth in the ever-evolving world of social media branding.

Taking Your Canva Skills to the Next Level

In this subchapter, we will explore how you can take your Canva skills to the next level and truly elevate your social media content creation. Whether you are a small business owner, freelance professional, marketing expert, content creator, student, nonprofit organization, corporate employee, brand manager, creative professional, or job seeker, mastering Canva is essential for creating visually appealing and engaging content.

To begin taking your Canva skills to the next level, consider exploring advanced design features and tools within the platform. Experiment with different fonts, colors, and layouts to create unique and eye-catching designs that stand out on social media. Utilize Canva's extensive library of design elements, templates, and stock photos to enhance your creations and make them truly professional and polished.

Another way to elevate your Canva skills is to learn more about design principles and techniques. Understanding concepts such as typography, color theory, and composition can help you create visually cohesive and impactful designs that resonate with your audience. Take the time to study design trends and best practices in social media content creation to stay current and relevant in your work.

Furthermore, consider expanding your Canva knowledge by exploring advanced features such as animation, video editing, and collaboration tools. These additional skills can help you create dynamic and engaging content that sets you apart from the competition. Take advantage of Canva's tutorials, webinars, and online resources to continue learning and growing as a Canva user.

In conclusion, by taking your Canva skills to the next level, you can unlock new opportunities for creating high-quality and engaging social media content. Whether you are a beginner or an experienced user, there is always room to grow and improve your design skills in Canva. Stay curious, keep experimenting, and never stop learning to become a master of Canva and elevate your social media content creation to new heights.

Appendix: Canva Keyboard Shortcuts and Tips for Efficiency

In this subchapter, we will explore the various keyboard shortcuts and tips that can help you work more efficiently in Canva. By mastering these shortcuts and implementing these tips, you will be able to create stunning social media content in a fraction of the time it would take using traditional methods.

Keyboard shortcuts are a great way to speed up your workflow in Canva. By memorizing these shortcuts, you can navigate the platform with ease and create your designs more quickly. Some commonly used keyboard shortcuts in Canva include Ctrl + C for copying, Ctrl + V for pasting, Ctrl + Z for undoing an action, and Ctrl + S for saving your work. By incorporating these shortcuts into your workflow, you can streamline the design process and save valuable time.

In addition to keyboard shortcuts, there are also several tips for efficiency in Canva that can help you optimize your workflow. One tip is to use templates as a starting point for your designs. Canva offers a wide range of professionally designed templates that you can customize to suit your needs. By starting with a template, you can save time and ensure that your designs are visually appealing and on-brand.

Another tip for efficiency in Canva is to organize your design elements using layers. By grouping similar elements together and organizing them into layers, you can easily make adjustments to specific parts of your design without affecting other elements. This can save you time and make the editing process much smoother.

By implementing these keyboard shortcuts and tips for efficiency in Canva, you can take your social media content creation to the next level. Whether you are a small business owner, freelance designer, marketing professional, student, nonprofit organization, corporate employee, brand manager, creative professional, or job seeker, mastering these techniques will help you create stunning designs in Canva with ease.

www.ingramcontent.com/pod-product-compliance
Lightning Source LLC
LaVergne TN
LVHW051609050326
832903LV00033B/4420